THE IMPACT OF CORRUPTION ON GROWTH AND DEVELOPMENT

Photo credit: freepik.com/free-photo

JClaude Germain, Ph.D.

THE IMPACT OF CORRUPTION

ON

GROWTH AND DEVELOPMENT *

JCLAUDE GERMAIN, PH.D.

*This text – revised and expanded – was originally submitted as a research paper at the end of a series of lectures on *Corruption* at **Harvard University** in the Summer of 2019.

ABOUT THE AUTHOR

J **Claude Germain** is a Ph.D. economist with a specialization in International Economics and Development Economics. He is a Harvard-educated professional in International Development and Environmental Policy, and Economic Growth. He is the author of *Trade Liberalization and Globalization, Poverty Reduction in the Least Developed Countries, The Impact of Corruption on Growth and Development,* and several articles on global issues.

Dr. Germain is a member of the International Economic Development Council (IEDC), and a lifetime member of the International Economics and Finance Society (IEFS). He had worked in the international community for over 14 years, and taught economics for over 12 years at the university level.

The author can be contacted via drjcgermain@gmail.com

ABSTRACT

JClaude Germain, Ph.D.

This study investigates the impact of corruption on growth and development at the global level and a country-specific level. It also investigates whether corruption "greases the wheels" or "sands the wheels" of the world's economies. To achieve the intended goal, the study uses worldwide data and country-specific data, Haiti being the country-specific case.

The empirical evidence strongly supports the view that corruption "sands the wheels" of economies across the globe. The study finds that corruption hinders growth and development in a variety of ways, and it costs the world economy an estimated $1 trillion paid in bribes every year, and $26 billion annually in stolen funds.

At a country-specific level, the study finds that corruption is endemic in Haiti, has impeded socio-economic development, and discourages foreign and domestic investments in the country. In 1977-8, for example, Haitian government misappropriation of funds represented 63% of government revenues. The consideration of two cases of corruption alone reveals that an estimated $504 million in the first case and $2 billion in the second were embezzled.

Keywords: corruption, growth, development, global phenomenon, United Nations Convention against Corruption, Transparency International, stolen assets recovery, Haiti.

TABLE OF CONTENTS

LIST OF TABLES

ACRONYMS

AFP	*Agence France Press* (France Press Agency)
AP	Associated Press
CSIS	Center for Strategic and International Studies
CPI	Corruption Perception Index
GDP	Gross Domestic Product
GNP	Gross National Product
IMF	International Monetary Fund
MINUJUSTH	French acronym for United Nations Mission for Justice Support in Haiti
NGO	Non-Governmental Organization
OAS	Organization of American States
OECD	Organization for Economic Cooperation and Development
OMRH	Office Management and Human Resources
PBS	Public Broadcasting System
StAR	Stolen Assets Recovery Initiative
TI	Transparency International
UN	United Nations
UNCAC	United Nations Convention against Corruption
UNDP	United Nations Development Programme
UNODC	United Nations Office on Drug and Crime

DEFINITIONS OF TERMS

Abuse of public property: the inappropriate use of public financial, human, and infrastructure resources.

Bribery: the act or practice of offering someone money, services, or something of value to persuade him or her to do something in return.

Corruption: 1) the misuse of entrusted power for private gain; 2) the abuse/misuse of power by government officials for private gain.

Cronyism (also called **clientelism**): mode of corruption where politicians are offered "bribes" with political support instead of cash, and supporters are, in turn, rewarded with jobs and government resources. In other words, it refers to favorable treatment of friends and associates in the distribution of resources and positions, regardless of qualifications.

Development: the process of improving the quality of all human lives and capabilities by raising people's levels of self-esteem, and freedom (Todaro & Smith).

Economic development: an economic transformation of a country or a region that leads to the improvement of the well-being and economic capabilities of its residents.

Economic growth: a persistent increase in per capita aggregate output and in the aggregate physical capital per worker in an economy.

Economic rent: a payment for the use of an economic resource above what is necessary for it to remain in its current use.

Embezzlement: misappropriation of entrusted property or funds for one's own use.

Extortion: Illegal use of one's official position or powers to obtain property, funds or information through the use of threat, often implicit, or the use of force.

Fraud: a deceptive practice used to obtain unfair advantage or unlawful gain.

Governance: there is not an agreed-upon definition because of the existence of different types of governance. For the purpose of this paper, governance is used in the sense of "good governance" as defined by the World Bank, meaning "the process in which authority is exercised in the management of a country's economic and social resources for development,... and the capacity of government to design, formulate and implement policies and discharge its function".

Growth: growth refers to the process or speed of increase in an activity, entity or quantity.

Insider trading: the use of information secured by an agent during a course of duty for personal gain.

Influence peddling (peddling influence): the solicitation of benefits by an individual in exchange for using one's influence to unfairly advance the interests of a particular person or party.

International asset recovery: the process by which the proceeds of corruption transferred abroad are recovered and repatriated to the country from which they were taken or to their rightful owners.

Kleptocracy: "Rule by thieves"; a form of government engaged in corruption and embezzlement to increase the personal wealth of government officials.

Money laundering: the depositing or transferring of money or the use of other means to conceal the source of unlawful transactions and to legitimize these activities.

Nepotism: a form of favoritism that involves family relationships.

Patronage: like clientelism (cronyism), patronage refers to the support or sponsorship by patrons in exchange for favors, such as appointments to governmental or political positions.

Rent-seeking: "spending time and money not to the production of real goods and services, but rather on trying to get the government to change the rules so as to make one's business more profitable". In economics, it is said that rent-seeking occurs when an individual, organization, or business tries to manipulate the economic and/or legal system to make money.

Transitional economies: economies in transition from a centrally planned economic system to a market-based economy, as in the former Soviet Union and many countries of Eastern Europe.

Transparency: Transparency International defines transparency as shedding light on shady deals, weak enforcement of rules and other illicit practices that undermine good governments, ethical businesses and society at large.

INTRODUCTION

Corruption – a complex and worldwide phenomenon – has existed for centuries and has been prevalent in both public (government) and private sectors. It occurs in all countries, developed as well as developing, rich and poor, but its impact varies depending on the country's culture, strength of institutions, political system, and stage of economic development. Two main definitions of corruption have been widely adopted: (1) the misuse of entrusted power for private gain, and (2) the abuse/misuse of power by government officials for private gain. The two definitions differ in the sense that the first one is broader because it encompasses both sectors (public and private) whereas the second one is limited to corruption by government officials and public servants. Regardless the definition, the United Nations Office on Drug and Crime (UNODC, 2016) views corruption as the single greatest obstacle to economic and social development around the world because it does not just steal money from where it is needed the most, it leads to weak governance, which in turn can fuel organized criminal networks and promotes crimes such as human trafficking, counterfeiting, arms and migrant smuggling. UNDP (2008) considers corruption as a governance issue, a failure of both institutions and the larger framework of social, judicial, political, and economic checks and balances needed to govern effectively.

Although corruption occurs in the private sector as well as the public sector and that some interaction or exchange between the two sectors exists, this study will focus on corruption in the public (government) sector. It will first examine corruption at the global level, and then at a country-specific level, using Haiti as a specific country to illustrate the impact of corruption on growth and development at a national level.

Before proceeding with the analysis of the impact of corruption on growth and development per se, it is important to point out that economic growth is a subset of economic development, which is a broader concept. The two concepts differ in terms of their scope, methods of measurement, and implications, *inter alia.* Although economic growth is a *sine qua non* condition for economic development, it is not a sufficient one. Growth can occur without generating development. That in part explains why development professionals and analysts have been more recently focusing on *inclusive* economic growth rather than conventional economic growth. "Inclusive growth" focuses not only on expanding a country's GDP per capita but also on "ensuring that the benefits of development reach the entire population, including the most vulnerable members".

There has been a debate on whether corruption "greases the wheels" or "sands the wheels" of economies worldwide, meaning whether it is beneficial or harmful. Although this paper will provide a critical analysis of the two opposing positions, it assumes that corruption has had negative effects on economic growth and development. Based on this premise, this research project will

1. investigate how has corruption undermined economic growth and development;
2. examine the measures adopted or proposed to mitigate the negative effects of corruption on growth and development; and

3. examine a country- specific case (Haiti) by analyzing the actions taken or suggested to address the negative impact of corruption on growth and development in that country.

This paper is structured as follows: section one (1) will examine corruption at the global level, establish the basis for the assumption made, provide information on a broad understanding of corruption, and consider some agreed-upon causes and consequences of corruption at the global level; section two (2) will focus on the state of corruption in Haiti, and then identify and analyze some domestic causes and consequences of corruption; section three (3) will consider Haitians' reactions to corruption; section four (4) will examine the anti-corruption measures adopted at the national level; and section five (5) will conclude the study.

CHAPTER 1
GLOBAL CORRUPTION

1.1. Basic Assumption

In the introduction, this study assumes that corruption has had negative effects on economic growth and development despite the debate on whether it is beneficial or harmful. To justify the assumption of a negative linkage between corruption and development, this paper will use scholarly work and findings of researchers/specialists in the field:

- The World Bank (1997) states that the roots of corruption lie deep in bureaucratic and political institutions, but while costs may vary and systemic corruption may coexist with strong economic performance, experience suggests that corruption is bad for development because it leads governments to intervene where they need not; and it undermines their ability to enact and implement policies in areas in which government intervention is clearly needed, such as healthcare and macroeconomic stability.
- Fisman and Golden (2017) posit that corruption carries negative consequences, and it harms economic efficiency,

increases social inequities, and undermines the functioning of democracy.

- The United Nations Development Programme (UNDP 2008) indicates that corruption has a negative impact on entrepreneurship partly because entrepreneurs and innovators require licenses and permits and paying bribes for these goods cut into profit margin. Furthermore, argues UNDP, corruption encourages risky practices, such as risky lending, and thus deters innovation by reducing economic growth in the long run.
- UNODC (2016) explains the negative impact of corruption when it states that corruption stifles economic growth, undermines the rules of law, and squanders talent and precious resources. Where corruption is rifle, continues UNODC, companies are reluctant to invest as the costs of doing business are significantly higher; it prevents people, countries, and businesses from fulfilling their potential, and it diverts funds intended to provide essential services. Furthermore, UNDOC quantifies the economic impact of corruption by indicating that every year $1 trillion is paid on bribes while an estimating $26 billion are stolen annually – a sum equivalent to more than 5 percent of the global GDP.

The afore-mentioned citations, inter alia, support the negative relationship between corruption and development and serve as the basis for the assumption made in this paper. However, it is important to note that the proponents of "efficient corruption" believe that corruption is beneficial. They argue that in some highly regulated countries without effective government institutions and governance systems, corruption can compensate for red tape and institutional weaknesses and 'grease the wheels' of the economy.

The above argument in support of corruption appears to have some validity, but it ignores the fact that corruption has been institutionalized precisely to perpetuate a practice that is very lucrative to corrupt officials and detrimental to the welfare of myriad of people within and across countries. The societal cost of corruption is so high that it outweighs the private gain of corrupt actors.

1.2 State of Global Corruption

Corruption has been a global phenomenon and a feature of public and private sectors within and across countries for centuries. Easterly (2002) cites some examples that illustrate the pervasiveness of this global phenomenon: (1) In **Japan**, a government prosecutor uncovered a scheme where businessmen who need a government favor would provide expensive free entertainment for the officials concerned; (2) in **Ecuador** in February 1997, agents for President Abdala Bucaram allegedly walked off with $3 million in Ecuadorian currency from the Central Bank shortly before his term of public office was to expire; (3) in **Korea**, four unqualified bone setters paid the equivalent of $11,000 to the Bureau of Health and Social Affairs in one province for fake licenses; (4) the former mayor of Beijing (**China**) and member of the Politburo, Chen Xitong, was sentenced to sixteen years in prison for allegedly diverting $2.2 billion in Beijing city funds during his time in public office, using kickbacks on construction contracts and many other devices; (5) in the **Philippines**, President Marcos initially promised to clean up corruption, but his lack of success can be measured in the zillions of dollars that he himself stole; (6) in **Zaire** [renamed Democratic Republic of Congo], President Mobutu Sese Seko, not satisfied with his personal fortune of billions of dollars, stole the entire gold-mining region of Kilo-moto, which covers 32,000 square miles and has reserves of 100 tons of gold.

According to Rose-Ackerman & Palifka (2016) the French oil company Elf [**France**] distributed at least 305 million euros in bribes around the world – in both developing and developed countries – to secure contracts to import oil between 1989 and 1993; in **Germany** bribes were apparently paid to win contracts worth DM 2.5 billion to build Terminal 2 at Frankfort Airport; a 2009 report in the **United Kingdom** revealed instances of 'gaming the expense system' with personal expenses unrelated to parliamentarians' work, resulting in prison sentences for members of the parliament.

With regard to the state of corruption during the socialist era in Eastern Europe, Fitzsimons (2007), using **Poland** and **Czech Republic** as examples, indicates that one popular Polish 'joke' of the time was 'They pretend to pay us: we pretend to work', and a saying among some industrial workers in former **Czechoslovakia** was 'if you don't rob the state, you rob your family'. The practice of corruption in Eastern Europe has not automatically disappeared with the end of the socialist era.

In Southern Europe, corruption has been widespread throughout the region. Foreign Policy (2013, July 16) reports that the former treasurer of **Spain**'s ruling center-right Popular Party (PP), Luis Barcenas, admitted in court to authoring handwritten ledgers detailing the secret flow of cash from private firms to top-level officials in the PP, and that Spanish Prime Minister Mariano Rajoy accepted regular payments from the illegal slush fund. Foreign Policy also indicates that according to Transparency International's Global Corruption Barometer 2013, perceptions of corruption and faith in government institutions are on the rise in the region, with 83 percent of respondents in **Greece**, 70 percent in **Italy**, and 66 percent in Spain claiming that 'government is run by a few big interest'. Regarding linkage between malfeasance and economic performance, Foreign Policy (2013) refers to "the common narrative these days about the connection between government corruption and economic stagnation in Europe's periphery". It also adds that few people believe their governments are effective in fighting grafts and that many blame this culture of corruption for the region's struggling economies.

In the **United States**, Lambsdorff (2007) mentions the case of Philadelphia's Department of Licenses and Inspections where officials accepted money from plumbing contractors in exchange for a quick approval of job-site work. In **Belgium** and the United Kingdom, Japan and Italy, Russia and Spain, and other countries, allegations of corruption play a more central role in politics today than at any time in recent memory (Klitgaard 1998).

The above citations and analysis illustrate the universality of corruption, which is rampant not only in countries in transition and developing countries but in developed countries as well. However, the fact that corruption is universal can be 'helpful' as well as 'unhelpful'. It is salutary because it helps us avoid unhelpful stereotypes; it is unhelpful because it may lead less discerning listeners or readers to the conclusion that because corruption exists in every country, nothing can be done about it where they live (Klitgaard, 1998).

Who participate in corruption?

According to Fisman and Golden (2017), there are four types of participants in corrupt activities: elected public officials, government bureaucrats, businesses, and ordinary citizens. The literature on corruption makes a distinction between "grand corruption" and "petty corruption". Petty corruption, also known as bureaucratic corruption, takes place at the implementation end of public services when public servants and the public interact; it involves low-level interactions between citizens, businesses, and government officials. Grand corruption, on the other hand, occurs at high levels of government, and it usually involves bribery and the embezzlement of huge sums of money or other public assets.

Corruption has been viewed by some social scientists as a "*multiple equilibrium*" phenomenon in society and an efficient tool to 'grease the wheels' of economies worldwide. As to why individuals agree to pay bribes, Fisman and Golden (2007) state that the decision to pay bribes reflects in large part what everyone expects everyone else to do; if others pay bribes, you will go along with them, and if everyone denounces bribery, you will do that instead. Fisman and Golden also argue that individuals pay bribes not because they necessarily have more relaxed moral compasses in high-corruption settings, but because it is too costly if their behavior deviates from the norms or expectations of those around them.

With regard to the view "grease the wheels" as an efficient tool, World Bank (2017) asserts that although in the short-term corruption may be able to 'grease the wheels of the economy', in the long term it negatively affects growth by diverting resources from more productive uses and negatively affects inequality by disproportionately benefiting those in power.

Fitzsimons (2007) argues that corruption is something of a conundrum to economists because the idea of 'unethical' behavior is difficult for economists to analyze given their assumption that all individuals and organizations simply pursue self-interest opportunistically. He also asserts that corruption has not always been viewed negatively by academics, and the popular view that 'grease money' was necessary in some way to the operation of business has been difficult to dismiss conclusively.

Few decades ago, academics espoused an "efficient corruption" view according to which bribery can allow an economy to grow in the presence of "bad" laws or regulations that put sand in the gears of market functioning (Fisman & Golden, 2017). In the same vein, Mauro (1995) reports that some authors suggested that corruption might *raise* economic growth, through two types of mechanisms: first, corrupt practices such as 'speed money' would enable individuals to avoid bureaucratic delay; second, government employees who are allowed to levy bribes would work harder, especially in the case where bribes act as a "piece rate". However, in his famous paper "Corruption and Growth", Mauro (1995) has provided evidence that corruption lowers economic growth via lower investment. After rigorously testing the claims in favor of corruption, Mauro concludes that the negative association between corruption and investment, as well as growth, is significant in both a statistical and an economic sense.

Proponents of "efficient corruption", however, had even defended kleptocracy, a form of government where corruption is rampant at highest levels. Weil (2013) notes that some economists argued that Kleptocracy could be conducive to economic growth because even a ruler who has no interest in the country's economy other than what can be stolen from it will still want the country to be as prosperous as possible, so that there is more to steal. This is a theoretical and argumentative position. In practice the priority of kleptocrats is not the prosperity of the State but misappropriation of public assets for their personal enrichment. Their principal interest is not to enlarge the pie but to appropriate a larger slice even if the pie is shrinking. As Rose-Ackerman & Palifka (2016) have indicated, corrupt rulers support policies that produce personalized gains even if they result in lower overall social wealth. (See box 1 for more information on kleptocrats).

Box 1. Kleptocrats' Behavior

"Taxes, regulations, subsidies, price fixing, and privatizations are examples of public- sector-activities that kleptocrats can manipulate for their own benefits. Because tax breaks can be awarded to corruption individuals and firms in return for bribes, kleptocrats may set high nominal tax rates to encourage payoffs. They may set heavy duties on necessities used by the poor and exempt luxuries. Kleptocrats view the regulatory system as a source of personal profits. Thus, regulations and licensing requirements may be imposed that have no justification other than to create a bottleneck that firms will pay to avoid. Efficient regulatory reforms will be opposed by the kleptocrat

> if the reforms would convert illegal into legal pricing systems. The kleptocrat will focus subsidies on individuals and business firms willing to pay them. Of course, even corrupt autocrats may need to satisfy the mass of population in order to maintain power, but they will also promulgate programs that induce the wealthy to pay for benefits". (Rose-Ackerman & Palifka, 2016)

Bribery, for example, was considered as an integral part of doing business and a way to "grease the wheels" of economies. In fact, most European countries used to allow business owners to deduct the amount of money paid in bribes as business expenses. These informal payments to public officials to facilitate enterprises' operations are in fact an illegal tax ("bribes tax") that increases operating costs, which are passed on to end-users of the product or service in the form of higher prices. Until recently, many scholars (and many organizations, including the World Bank) saw anti-corruption efforts as a distraction to the "real" problems holding back economic development (Fisman and Golden, 2017). The World Bank still holds a different view of corruption and how to approach it despite its recognition that corruption has a negative impact on development. For instance, it defines corruption as "a deals-based way to sustain agreements among certain individuals or groups" (World Bank 2017).

Although some economists and international institutions were reluctant to tackle the problem of corruption, it is comforting to acknowledge that many of them have been more recently addressing the topic during the last three decades, and have even shared the view that corruption has had adverse consequences on economic development. In this regard, Krugman & Obstfeld (2006) state that government regulations that promote corruption harm economic prosperity, and statistical studies have found that corruption tends to have net negative effects on economic efficiency and growth. Some economists have even advocated for the elimination of corruption. For instance, Todaro & Smith (2017) argue that the elimination of corruption is important for development because honest government may promote growth and sustainably high incomes. They further assert that the effects of corruption fall disproportionately on the poor and are a major restraint on their ability to escape from poverty.

Arguing against some economists' notion that corruption in the form of bribery represents a mutually "desirable and beneficial exchange", Lambsdorff (2007) replies that this notion disregards how corruption constrains decision-making, and when officials cannot credibly promise to reject side-payments from clients, they are not trustworthy at the outset; and concludes that corruption turns out to be harmful even to those who have the chance of striking illegal deals.

During the last few decades, corruption has been analyzed very closely, and more studies have been conducted on the issue, which has helped to shift the view on the topic. There is now a "near-consensus" that corruption is harmful in the sense that its high costs degrade public trust and impede economic development. International institutions – including the World Bank, the Organization of American States (OAS), the Organization for the Economic Cooperation and Development (OECD) - that used to ignore, if not dismiss, the negative impact of corruption, have embarked on a mission to control worldwide corruption. Former World Bank's president, Jim Yong Kim, declared corruption a "public enemy number one" for developing countries. The World Bank Group has decided to tackle the issue of corruption because it represents a major challenge to the attainment of its goals of "ending extreme poverty by 2030 and boosting shared prosperity for the poorest 40 percent of people in developing countries".

Combating corruption, however, is a monumental and intricate task because corruption is a systemic, entrenched and (almost) invisible phenomenon that permeates the world in different forms. In some of the most complex and difficult forms to break, states De Souza Martins (1996), politicians both receive bribes and make disbursements to companies in complex corruption structures such as those that existed in many South American countries, where the line between private and public activities of politicians was often blurred in a system of traditional patronage.

As the saying goes "You cannot manage what you cannot measure". (More on measurement later in this paper). Nevertheless, the fight against corruption is a *sine qua* non condition in the quest for economic growth and development in the developing world.

1.3. Forms of Corruption

Government corruption takes many forms, from a tax inspector who accepts a bribe to overlook income on which he is supposed to collect taxes, to a mayor who trades city contracts for cash payments, all the way up to a president who grants a lucrative monopoly to his son (Weil 2014).

The most common forms of corruption are bribery, embezzlement, extortion, cronyism (also called clientelism), abuse of public property, fraud, influence peddling (peddling influence), insider trading, nepotism, money laundering, patronage, and speed money. In the public sector, corruption is labelled as "petty" or "grand". As previously stated, petty corruption refers to low-level corruption that occurs when bureaucrats interact with the public, and grand corruption is corruption that involves high-level political and government officials.

As one of the main tools of corruption, bribery occurs in the public sector when government officials solicit, accept, or extort bribes, and private agents offer bribes to circumvent public policies. Theft (an abuse of public property) is another common form of corruption. In this case, public officials responsible for the management of state assets simply steal them. World Bank (1997) asserts that theft of financial resources is a common practice in which officials may pocket tax revenues or fees (often with the collusion of the payer, in effect combining theft and bribery), steal cash from treasuries, extend advances to themselves that are never repaid, or draw pay for fictitious 'ghosts' workers.

1.4. Causes and Consequences of Corruption

The causes and consequences of corruption are numerous, complex, and concerning.

1.4.1. Causes of Corruption

Klitgaard (1988) has summed up his view on the causes of corruption in the formula:

C = M + D – A (corruption equals monopoly plus discretion minus accountability). According to this view, monopoly increases corruption, discretion causes corruption, and accountability reduces corruption. Although Klitgaard 's formula has been considered classical, some analysts have critiqued the idea of a "corruption formula". Stephenson (2014), for example, argues that "while Klitgaard is indisputably right that some corruption arises because unaccountable officials have the sole power to make discretionary decisions, framing this point as a 'formula' –which implies that it is an immutable law – is inaccurate and misleading". According to Stephenson, tight controls based on formal criteria leave little room for individual officials to make discretionary judgment calls.

According to World Bank (1997) the causes of corruption are always contextual, rooted in a country's policies, bureaucratic traditions, political development and social history, but tends to flourish when institutions are weak and government policies generate economic rents. Low civil service salary has also been mentioned as a major cause of corruption because it reduces the incentive of public employees to work productively and efficiently.

In this sense it has had an adverse impact on economic growth and development.

Why is civil service salary kept low?

With regard to the issue of low salaries, World Bank (1997) states that in some countries pay levels may always have been low, with the formal understanding that staff will find their own ways to supplement inadequate pay. This is indeed a clear example of institutionalized corruption, which impedes development in several countries. The World Bank (1997) further indicates that dysfunctional government budgets, inadequate supplies and equipment, delays in the release of budget funds (including pay) may demoralize staff, and the motivation to remain honest may be further weakened if senior officials and political leaders who resist corruption lack protection.

Low job opportunities, lack of strict and fast punishments, lack of transparency, lack of independent detective agency, lack of state funding to elections, lack of enough powers to the judicial system, and encouragement of unhealthy competition have also been recognized as causes of corruption.

1.4.2. Consequences of Corruption

UNDP (2008) enumerates the following consequences of corruption: (1) corruption exacerbates poverty and negatively affects economic growth; (2) corruption has a disproportionate impact on women; (3) corruption has a debilitating effect on development in countries rich in natural resources; (4) corruption encourages conflict and is an obstacle to consolidating peace; (5) corruption undermines the delivery of humanitarian and reconstruction assistance; (6)corruption shares a nexus with organized crime in its various forms, in many countries; (7) corruption violates human rights; and (8) corruption fosters an anti-democratic environment characterized by uncertainty, unpredictability, declining moral and ethical values and disrespect for constitutional institutions and authority.

In terms of the relationship between corruption and development, UNDP argues that corruption hinders economic growth because it discourages foreign and domestic investment by increasing opportunity for rent-seeking, creating uncertainty and reducing incentives for both foreign and domestic investors. As consequences of corruption, UNDP (2008) reports the following:

- More than $1 trillion ($ 1,000 billion) are paid in bribes every year, over 3 percent of world income in 2002 (World Bank Institute estimate).
- More than 70 percent of small-and medium-sized Enterprises (SMEs) in transition economies perceive corruption as an impediment to their business (Business Environment and Enterprise Performance Survey, 2000).
- $ 148 billion leaves the African continent every year because of corruption (African Union estimates).
- In Italy, a modest reduction in corruption would increase growth by 0.3 percentage points, even with unchanged investment (Collier and Hoeffer 2005).
- In Latin America, reducing corruption to the level of Costa Rica would reduce operating costs in electricity by 23 percent (Collier and Hoeffer 2005).
- The amount of money extorted and stolen each year from developing countries is over 10 times the approximately $100 billion in foreign assistance being provided to them by all the governments and civil society organizations in the world (Nazario, 2007).

UNDP also indicates that globally, a modest reduction in corruption would increase investment in telecommunications by 0.8 percentage points.

UNDP, however, has qualified its position by stating that the fact that corruption is correlated with poverty, poor service delivery and other negative phenomena does not necessarily mean that corruption causes them, but there is little dispute that corruption and poverty go hand in hand.

Using available estimates for some national economies, Fitzsimons (2007) provides some information on the direct costs of corruption in table 1.

Table 1. Direct Costs of Corruption

Description	Costs	Source
Fraud	$600 billion in USA in 2002 (6% of revenues annually).	Association of Certified Fraud Examiners (2004);
	Some estimates show 20% rate likely based on employee surveys.	Ernst & Young (2002)
Bribery	$1 trillion annually (global) from 2001-2 data	World Bank (2004)

Source: Fitzsimons (2007). In *Corruption and Development: The Anti-Corruption Campaigns* p.56

Several economists, such as Mauro 1995; Tanzi 1997; Gupta 2000, indicate that corruption has a negative impact on economic growth because it distorts incentives and market forces, diverts talent and resources towards 'lucrative' rent-seeking activities, and acts as an inefficient tax on business, which increases production costs and reduces the profitability of investments.

Corruption has also negatively impacted economic performance by lowering productivity – the amount of output per unit of input achieved by a firm, industry, or country. Studies conducted by researchers such as Lambsdorff (2003) found repeated support for corruption lowering the productivity of capital. Linking corruption to productivity more directly, Lambsdorff (2003) indicates that an increase in corruption by one point on a scale from 10 (highly clean) to 0 (highly corrupt) lowers productivity by 2 percent, and an improvement with regard to corruption by 6 points of the Transparency International Corruption Perception Index increases GDP by more than 10 percent of the total capital stock.

The inverse relationship between corruption and productivity further underscores the importance of curbing corruption because productivity is a significant determinant of living standard. By lowering productivity, corruption *ipso facto* decreases people's standard of living, which is an impediment to growth and development.

With regard to the impact of corruption and tax evasion on development, Stuart Yikona and a team of researchers at the World Bank conducted a study on "ill-gotten money" in Malawi and Namibia (two African countries) between November 2010 and February 2011. They estimated that tax revenue actually collected by the Government of Malawi Revenue Authority is only 22% of the GDP. If the national tax authority, add Yikona and the team, had successfully collected all the taxes it was due, government revenue would increase by 50 percent, which approximates the amount Malawi receives in foreign aid (11.7 percent of Malawi GDP). The study also reveals that uncollected taxes in Namibia are equivalent to about 9 percent of the GDP. These uncollected taxes are directly attributed to corruption ("ill-gotten money"), which has had negative impacts on the economies of the two countries.

1.5 Actions and Solutions

Combating corruption is such a difficult and sensitive issue that many national political leaders who support such efforts in principle are hesitant to undertake them in practice (Klitgaard 1998). As "grease the wheels" was (is) a *modus operandi*, most national political leaders are indeed reluctant to fight corruption because they do not want to become victims of their own initiatives. They believe that fighting corruption is not only difficult but also costly and even dangerous. The experience of Luis Inacio Lula da Silva, former president of Brazil, sent chills through the spines of several would-be political corruption fighters, especially in the developing world. The strategy "fry a few big fish" is a laudable one, but it is a double-edged sword ; it does send a clear signal to corrupt leaders that the days of the insidious practice "grease the wheels" is no longer acceptable, but it may also prevent them from joining the fight because they might have dirty clothes in their closets.

As almost all members of Brazil' s political elite have been exposed as deeply involved in large-scale corruption (Fisman & Golden, 2017), in May 2003 President Lula (as he is better known) initiated an anti-corruption program to discourage the misuse of public funds by public administrators. In launching the program, President Lula said: "I Think the Brazilian society needs to understand once and for all, that we are only going to be able to truly fight corruption when the civil society, with the instruments made available, can act as a watch dog" (Finan & Ferraz 2005). After leaving the presidency, however, President Lula was imprisoned after being convicted for "corruption and money laundering".

As national political leaders are reluctant to tackle the issue of corruption, which is a global phenomenon with disastrous socio-economic consequences, what has the international community done or proposed to do to combat this ubiquitous scourge at both national and international levels?

Preventing and combating corruption, argues UNODC (2016), requires a comprehensive approach, but only in a climate of transparency, accountability, and participation by all members of society is this possible. Klitgaard (1998) recommends the following approaches:

1. *Punish some major offenders.* To this end, he states that successful strategies begin by 'frying a few big fish'; (2) *Involve the*

people in diagnosing corrupt systems, and posits that successful campaigns against corruption involve the people because citizens, if consulted, are fertile sources of information about where corruption is occurring; (3) *Focus on Prevention by repairing corrupt systems,* and he notes that successful anti-corruption efforts fix corrupt systems; (4) *Reform Incentives.* In many countries, says Klitgaard, public sector wages are so low that a family cannot survive on a typical official's salary. To create incentives, he emphasizes the need for an "overhauling of pay schemes".

As the World Bank views corruption "as a deals-based way to sustain agreements among certain individuals or groups", it has a more nuanced approach to the phenomenon. World Bank (2017) indicates that anti-corruption strategies that assume that aggregate levels of corruption can be reduced through a top-down combination of policies that improve enforcement of rule of law, change the expected returns to corruption (for example, through bureaucratic pay increases, greater transparency, or harsher punishments) are wrong and have generally delivered modest reductions in corruption. It believes that these strategies must tackle the underlying reasons that are related to systemic features in the policy arena such as entrenched power structures or social norms in order to achieve significant control of corruption. But how to implement such a cumbersome and overpowering approach?

To combat corruption worldwide, certain conventions have been adopted and agreements reached at the international level. Among them are Organization for Economic Co-operation and Development Convention on Combatting Bribery of Foreign Public Officials in International Business; Inter-American Convention against Corruption; African Union Convention on Preventing and Combating Corruption; Financial Action Task Force (FATF) on Money Laundering; the World Bank Group's International

Corruption Hunters Alliance (ICHA; Transparency International; and the United Nations Convention against Corruption. This study will focus on the last two.

1.5.1. Transparency International

As a global organization that works with governments, businesses, and citizens, Transparency International (TI) envisages to "stop the abuse of power, bribery and secret deals". Since 1995, TI has been publishing every year a Corruption Perception Index (CPI) that serves as a global indicator of perceived levels of corruption in the public sector of countries and territories across the world. The Index ranks countries and territories by allocating a score to each one: from zero (0), meaning highly corrupt, to 100, very clean. For instance, Transparency International (2019) measures public sector corruption in 180 countries and territories, which reveals that the top countries are New Zealand and Denmark, with a score of 87 each, Finland with a score of 86, and Singapore, Sweden, and Switzerland with a score of 85 each; the bottom countries are Somalia, South Sudan, and Syria with scores of 9, 12, and 13 respectively, which are followed by Yemen with a score of 15, and Venezuela, Sudan, Equatorial Guinea and Afghanistan with a score of 16 each.

Commenting on the state and consequences of corruption, Huguette Labelle, Chair of Transparency International, states that the 2007 "Global Corruption Barometer [GCB] has made it clear that too often people must part with their-hard-earned money to pay for services that should be free".

TI (2019) also states that a majority of countries show little to no improvement in tackling corruption, which is more pervasive in countries where big money can flow freely into electoral campaigns and where governments listen only to the wealthy or well-connected individuals.

Table 2 provides statistical data compiled by tradingeconomics.com on the level of perceived corruption in the Group of 20 for

2018 and 2019. The Group of 20, referred to as G-20, is a group of finance ministers and central bank governors from 19 of the world's largest economies, which include several developing countries, and the European Union (EU). The G-20's mandate is to promote global economic growth, international trade, and regulation of financial markets.

Table 2. G-20 Corruption Perception Index

Country	2019 Score	2018 Score
Argentina	45	40
Australia	77	77
Brazil	35	35
Canada	77	81
China	41	39
France	69	72
Germany	80	80
India	41	41
Indonesia	40	38
Italy	53	52
Japan	73	73
Mexico	29	28
Netherlands	82	82
Russia	28	28
Saudi Arabia	53	49
Singapore	85	85
South Africa	44	43
South Korea	59	57
Spain	62	58
Switzerland	85	85
Turkey	39	41
United Kingdom	77	80
United States	69	71

Source: tradingeconomics.com/country-list/corruption-index?continent=g20

The CPI scores in Table 2 appears to corroborate the TI's assertion that a majority of countries show little or no improvement in tackling corruption. From 2018 to 2019, the level of perceived corruption has remained unchanged in nine (9) of the 19 G-20 countries: Australia, Brazil, Germany, India, Japan, Netherlands, Russia, Singapore, and Switzerland. The reported scores for China, Indonesia, Italy, Mexico, South Africa, South Korea, and Spain reveal slight improvements, more for some than others (see Table 2). As per the Corruption Perception Index, Canada, France, Turkey, United Kingdom, and the United States have lost ground in curbing corruption. Their scores have dropped from 81 to 77, 72 to 69, 41 to 38, 80 to 77, and 71 to 69 respectively. Amid the Group, the two least corrupt nations are Singapore and Switzerland with a score of 85 each, and the two most corrupt ones are Russia and Brazil with low scores of 28 and 35 respectively.

Regarding the Corruption Perception Index (CPI), it is important to emphasize the importance of the middle word "Perception" to dispel any confusion that might arise between "actual" and "perceived" corruption. The actual level of corruption is unknown because corruption is usually "invisible to outsiders". Bribery for instance, is mainly a cash transaction. No records are kept, no receipts are given, and usually no paper trail exists.

Fisman & Golden (2017) indicate that where corruption relies on electronic bank transfers to move and launder money, the funds are sanitized so the movements do not alert authorities. They further assert that in cases of large-scale and high-level corruption, officials routinely use shell to move money out of the country. The difficulty of exact measurement is the rationale for the use of "Corruption Perceptions Index", which is an index created by Transparency International to rank countries "by their perceived levels of public sector corruption, as determined by expert assessments and opinion surveys".

In addition to corruption within their borders, several countries export corruption via bribery. To monitor foreign bribery by country of origin, Transparency International also devises a "Bribery Payers Index" and ranks each country after conducting a *Bribe Payers Survey* of over 3,000 business executives worldwide. A score is then assigned to each country based on the views of the business executives "on the extent to which companies from 28 of the world's leading economies engage in bribery when doing business abroad". According to Transparency International, the 28 countries and territories in the *Bribe Payers Index* were selected based on the value of their Foreign Direct Investment (FDI) outflows, the value of their exports; the index includes all G-20 countries.

Table 3 shows the Bribe Payers Index (BPI) for 2011, based on a scale of 0 to 10. A maximum score of 10 corresponds with the view that companies from that country *never* engage in bribery abroad, and a score of zero (0) indicates that companies from that country *always* engage in bribery abroad.

Table 3. Bribe Payers Index 2011

RANK	COUNTRY/TERRITORY	SCORE	NUMBER OF OBSERVATIONS
1	Netherland	8.8	273
2	Switzerland	8.8	244
3	Belgium	8.7	221
4	Germany	8.6	576
4	Japan	8.6	319
6	Australia	8.5	168
6	Canada	8.5	209
8	Singapore	8.3	256
8	United Kingdom	8.3	414
10	United States	8.1	651
11	France	8.0	435
11	Spain	8.0	326

(*Continued*)

Table 3. (*Continued*)

RANK	COUNTRY/TERRITORY	SCORE	NUMBER OF OBSERVATIONS
13	South Korea	7.9	152
14	Brazil	7.7	163
15	Hong Kong	7.6	208
15	Italy	7.6	397
15	Malaysia	7.6	148
15	South Africa	7.6	191
19	Taiwan	7.5	193
19	India	7.5	168
19	Turkey	7.5	139
22	Saudi Arabia	7.4	138
23	Argentina	7.3	115
23	United Arab Emirates	7.3	156
25	Indonesia	7.1	153

Source: Transparency International

Table 3 also ranks Mexico as #26 with a score of 7.0, and 121 observations; China #27 with a score of 6.5, and 608 observations; Russia #28 with a score of 6.1, and 172 observations.

The Index shows that all the 28 counties are involved in bribery in foreign countries but some at a lesser extent than others. For instance, a score of 8.8 for each the Netherlands and Switzerland indicates that companies from those countries are less likely to engage in bribery abroad than companies from Russia with a score of 6.1 and China with a score of 6.5. In other words, companies from the last two countries are more willing to engage in bribery overseas than the first two.

1.5.2. The United Nations Convention Against Corruption

The United Nations Convention against Corruption (UNCAC) was adopted by the UN General Assembly on 31 October 2003, and entered into force on 4 December 2005. According to Article 1, the purposes of the Convention are:

a To promote and strengthen measures to prevent and combat corruption more efficiently and effectively;
b To promote, facilitate and support international cooperation and technical assistance in the prevention of and fight against corruption, including in asset recovery;
c To promote integrity, accountability and proper management of public affairs and public policy.

Under this Convention, countries are bound to render specific forms of mutual legal assistance in gathering and transferring evidence for use in court, to extradite offenders; furthermore, it requires countries to establish criminal offences to cover a wide variety of acts of corruption, if these are not already crimes under domestic law (UNODC, 2019).

UNCAC covers five principal areas: (1) preventive measures; (2) criminalization and law enforcement; (3) international cooperation; (4) asset recovery; and (5) technical assistance and information exchange. It also covers several forms of corruption, including bribery, and "abuse of functions". Fighting corruption has, therefore, become a priority because corruption hinders economic growth and development by discouraging investments (both foreign and domestic).

In order to recover stolen assets, the World Bank Group and the United Nations Office on Drugs and Crimes (UNODC) have formed a partnership called the Stolen Asset Recovery Initiative (StAR) whose purpose is to support "international efforts to end safe havens for corrupt funds". StAR works with developing countries and financial centers to prevent the laundering of the proceeds of corruption and to facilitate more systematic and timely return of stolen assets (World Bank, 2020). This international cooperation to recover stolen funds and restore them to their "rightful owners" is a powerful tool in the fight against corruption because it may serve as a deterrent to corrupt public officials from this lucrative personal endeavor, and foster economic development.

In the fight against global corruption, it is worth mentioning the passage of the Foreign Corrupt Practices Act of 1977, a U.S Federal law that prohibits U.S. citizens and entities from bribing government officials overseas. This law was enacted, in part, as a response to a scandal involving Japanese politicians "who accepted bribes to approve contracts to buy U.S. military aircraft". This law is now in jeopardy because the current U.S President, Donald J. Trump, considers the 1977 Act "unfair" to U.S companies. In fact, The New York Times, dated January 15, 2020, reports that "President Trump wanted to strike down a law that prohibits companies from bribing foreign officials, calling the ban 'so unfair' to American companies [and he] asked administration officials to help kill the Foreign Corrupt Practices Act…". The president believes that U.S companies should be allowed to pay bribes to get business overseas. To that end, the White House Economic Adviser, Larry Kudlow, has indicated that the Trump administration is "looking at" making changes to the 1977 anti-bribery law. The weakening or repeal of the Act would be a setback for the anti-corruption movement. Although the 1977 Act has not completely eliminated bribery by U.S. companies overseas, it has contributed to decrease its intensity. The 2011 Bribe Payers Index shows that the United States ranked number 10 with a score of 8.1, which makes it less likely to engage in bribery overseas in comparison to many other countries (see Table 3).

The weakening or repeal of the 1977 Act, however, would represent a dilemma for the United States - as a member of the global community - because Article 16 of the United Nations Convention against Corruption, dealing with *Bribery of foreign public officials and officials of public international organizations* prohibits bribery of foreign public officials. Paragraph 1 of the said Article of the Convention that went into force in 2005 stipulates, "Each State Party shall adopt such legislative and other measures as may be necessary to establish as a criminal offence, when committed intentionally, the promise, offering or giving to a foreign public official or an official of a public international organization, directly or indirectly, of an undue advantage, for the official himself or herself or another person or entity, in order that the official act or refrain from acting in the exercise of his or her official duties, in order to obtain or retain business or other undue advantage in relation to the conduct of international business". Article 15 of the Convention also criminalizes "*bribery of national public officials*". Will the United States resort to *rapport de forces* - the influence, power and efficacy of the parties involved - to bypass or ignore UNCAC?

Corruption is to growth and development what COVID-19 (corona virus disease 2019) is to human life, particularly in developing countries. Whereas COVID-19 is a global pandemic attacking human health, corruption is also a global pandemic attacking people's economic health. Both phenomena are ubiquitous and have disastrous impacts. The obvious interconnectedness between human health and economic health underscores the importance of neutralizing the negative effects of both pandemics for the welfare of humanity.

1.5.3. Recovery of Stolen Assets

How successful has been **StAR** in recovering stolen assets and restoring them to their "prior legitimate owners"?

According to World Bank Group (2020), the Initiative to recover stolen assets has not been as successful as it could have been "despite the advances in international efforts since the United Nations Convention against Corruption went into force" in 2005 because of many barriers. The World Bank has identified some of the barriers as follows: 1) lack of political will to investigate and charge corrupt officials; 2) a dearth of capacity, expertise, and resources to pursue cases or cooperate internally; and 3) the existence of a global financial system that enables corrupt officials to rapidly move and conceal illicit funds. In order to circumvent the erected barriers, World Bank Group (2020) "offers a rarely used way to recover the proceeds of corruption – insolvency proceedings- thus contributing to the development of an additional tool for the realization of the UNCAC's principle on asset recovery".

The insolvency proceedings were successful in the case *Federal Republic of Brazil and Municipality of Sao Paulo vs. Durant International Ltd and Kildare Finance Ltd.* Brazil and Sao Paulo won the case and Durant and Kildare were ordered to pay $30 million to Brazil and Sao Paulo, and the plaintiffs recovered $2.1 million. (For more information on *insolvency proceedings* and the case, see *Going for Broke* by World Bank Group). With regard to the proceedings, it is worth noting that the insolvency mechanisms can be used against bribe takers as well as bribe payers.

Following the fall of President Zine el Abidine Ben Ali of Tunisia, $ 29 million was recovered from a Lebanese bank account belonging to the former President's wife; a plane, yachts, and other physical assets were also returned to Tunisia; furthermore, the Government of Liechtenstein returned US$225 million to Nigeria, following fourteen years of legal maneuvering (https://blogs.worldbank.org/governance/recovering-stolen-assets-road-ending-impunity). The Initiative has had other limited successes. **StAR** has assisted in the freezing or recovery of over $1 billion in stolen funds, and the return of $321 million of recovered assets to Nigeria (World Bank 2020).

The recovery of stolen assets after long and meticulous legal maneuvers is very encouraging and significant in the battle against corruption because it sends a powerful signal to corrupt officials that there is "no safe heavens" for embezzled public assets. Moreover, it can serve as a deterrent to would-be corrupt public officials who would like to hide misappropriated funds in foreign financial institutions, but some mechanisms need to be put in place to prevent the returned assets from being re-stolen. Thus, the question:

What happens to the recovered assets after being returned to their "prior legitimate owners"?

Article 51 of the United Nations Convention against Corruption states that the return of assets is a "fundamental principle" of the Convention. Article 54 sets the "*Mechanisms for recovery of property through international cooperation in Confiscation*". Article 55 addresses "*International cooperation for the purposes of confiscation*" of stolen assets. Article 57 deals with the issue of "*Return and disposal of assets*" by stating in part in paragraph 1: "Property confiscated by a State Party...shall be disposed of, including by return to its prior legitimate owners...by that State Party in accordance with the provisions of this Convention and its domestic law". UNCAC, however, is silent on the use of the recovered assets once returned to the country of origin because it would be considered too intrusive. In political and diplomatic circles, it would be viewed as "interference". It is imperative that the recovered assets be returned to their "prior legitimate owners", but a system should be put in place (or at least a binding agreement) on how the assets would be used to prevent them from being re-stolen. As each State Party is bound to the provisions of the Convention, perhaps Article 1 of the Convention could be used as a basis for such an agreement. Article 1 (c) stipulates (as one of the purposes of the Convention): "To promote integrity, accountability and *proper management* [emphasis] of public affairs and public property".

The recovered and returned stolen assets should be used for development, which would be conducive to an improvement in individuals' standard of living and quality of life. People in those affected countries are the real victims of corruption in the form of theft (financial and physical) and are, therefore, the "prior legitimate owners" of the returned assets.

CHAPTER 2
CORRUPTION IN HAITI

The general information on corruption provided at the global level in section one (1) will serve as a background against which corruption will be analyzed within Haiti's context because, as a member of the global community, the country exhibits the same features of corruption. Furthermore, Haiti – like other State Parties - is obligated to address the corruption issue once the United Nations Convention against Corruption entered into force.

2.1. Brief Profile of Haiti

Haiti, officially known as *Republique d'Haiti* (Republic of Haiti), occupies the western one-third of the island of Hispaniola, an area of 27,750 square kilometers, in the Caribbean (the Americas). It shares the island with the Dominican Republic, which occupies the eastern two-thirds. Haiti has two official languages: French and Haitian Creole, and has a population of approximately 11 million people. Port-au-Prince is the capital city. The country is very vulnerable to natural disasters, such as earthquakes, hurricanes, and floods.

Haiti is a free-market economy and *gourde* is its currency whose value is determined by the market via the floating exchange rate system. Haiti's economy has been experiencing a 'dollarization' phenomenon in recent years because many domestic transactions have been carried out in U.S. dollars instead of Haitian *gourdes* (Germain 2010). The country has a presidential-parliamentary political system, meaning the President has to share power with a Prime Minister he or she designates, but the nomination must be ratified by the parliament. In other words, the President is elected directly by the people, which in theory means he or she is under direct voters' control and is accountable to them, but the unelected Prime Minister is accountable to the parliament that can at will give him or her a vote of no confidence. This system of governance - adopted after the Duvalier dynasty to prevent the repetition of dictatorship and president for life - encourages conflict and corruption, and fuels political instability because it has often been used as a tool for political bargaining and extracting favors. In fact, it largely explains why the country is presently in a political imbroglio – a "dissolved" parliament and a president governing by decrees.

2.2. State of Corruption in Haiti

Before going into the analysis of the state of corruption, this paper provides in table 4 below some statistical data on the level of perceived corruption in the country.

Based on the data in table 4, Haiti's corruption perceptions index (CPI), which relates to the level of corruption as seen by business people and country analysts, was 20 in 2018. The Index reflects a range between 100 (highly clean) and 0 (highly corrupt). A score of 20 out of 100 does indicate a high level of perceived corruption. As the table shows, Haiti's corruption perceptions index has varied between a score of 14 and 22, reaching a high of 22 out of 100 in 2017 and a low of 14 in 2008. Using the score for each of the 12 years, this author has calculated an average score of 18.66 for the 12-year period, which indicates the state of perceived corruption in the country throughout the period.

Table 4. Haiti: Corruption Perceptions Index (2007 – 2018)

DATE	VALUE	CHANGE, %
2018	20.00	-9.09 %
2017	22.00	10.00 %
2016	20.00	17.65 %
2015	17.00	-10.53 %
2014	19.00	0.00 %
2013	19.00	0.00 %
2012	19.00	5.56 %
2011	18.00	-18.19 %
2010	22.00	22.22 %
2009	18.00	28.57 %
2008	14.00	-12.50 %
2007	16.00	

Source: Corruption Perceptions Index by Transparency International, 2018

According to the Center for Strategic and International Studies (CSIS, 2018), a network of corruption permeates all sectors of the country's public governance, including all political institutions and the ensuing human capital and economic ecosystem. CSIS also acknowledges that several Haitian governments have attempted to address the corruption problem but without success despite a significant commitment by a wide spectrum of the international community since the 1980s.

According to Klitgaard (2010), systemic corruption is one of Haiti's realities; it has undercut the provision of social services, the efficiency of ports and electricity, revenue agencies, the construction and maintenance of roads, and the system of justice – not to mention Haitian politics. Systemic corruption is the biggest obstacle to economic growth and development in Haiti. As reported by Klitgaard (2010), Haiti Prime Minister Michele Duvivier Pierre-Louis has diagnosed the problem in a July 2009 interview as follows:

> All the elites – the mulatto elites, the university elites, the union elites, the peasant elites – are like a huge elephant sitting on this country and you cannot move it, because there are no [functioning] political parties, and everyone becomes corrupted and perverted. If you can't go into that system, the system rejects you. And so far, we have not found the wrench that will move this thing.

The system wasted no time to respond to the Prime Minister's comments. She was vehemently criticized by the "political class and a largely corrupt economic elite", and as a result she lost her political support. Ironically, the political elite used corruption as a cover to justify their attacks on her. Widespread rumors said that part of $197 million in aid following the 2008 hurricanes had disappeared (Klitgaard 2010), and they blamed her, as head of government, for the alleged disappearance of the missing funds.

The campaign against Prime Minister Pierre-Louis was not a campaign against corruption per se, it was *au contraire* a campaign against anti-corruption. As the system was threatened, she had to be sacrificed to preserve the status quo. On October 29, 2009, the Haitian Senate voted to dismiss her and her government, and she was removed from office (Klitgaard 2010). The removal of Prime Minister Pierre-Louis does confirm the veracity of her statement "If you can't go into that system, the system rejects you". (The system of government in Haiti has a domestic facet and a foreign facet as well, but the second one is beyond the purview of this work.)

With regard to the state of corruption under the current administration of President Moise, CSIS states that it started badly with the president himself being accused of money laundering even before his inauguration in February 2017, but President Moise muddied the waters further by subsequently firing the head of the government unit investigating the allegations.

2.3 Causes of Corruption in Haiti

In addition to the causes identified at the international level, which also apply to Haiti, *Le Nouvelliste* (2018, November 27) has examined four causes that specifically impact the country:

- *Inefficacite et manque de ressources des institutions publiques* (Inefficiency of public institutions and their lack of resources).

Le Nouvelliste indicates that the inefficiency of public institutions and their lack of resources is one of the causes and consequences of corruption in Haiti. Citing BRIDES (2007) it adds that public administration in Haiti is considered ineffective not only by citizens but also by state employees who have given a maximum score of 2.7 out of 10 to the ability of public institutions to provide services to the population.

- **Informality**

Another cause of corruption identified by *Le Nouvelliste is* informality, which takes precedence over laws and procedures established especially in financial institutions where a large part of the budget is carried out through inappropriate channels. The newspaper substantiates its arguments via this example: in 1999-2000, the National Palace managed funds for a large number of projects in sectors as diverse as agriculture, roads, and housing, which has converted the Presidency into an investment institution. This is an excellent opportunity to embezzle funds because the Presidency is accountable to nobody.

- **Dysfunction of the Judiciary**

Le Nouvelliste argues that linked to informality and lack of resources, the dysfunction of the judiciary is the principal cause of corruption in Haiti, and that the Haitian judicial system has the least reliable institutions, which, in the opinion of those interviewed in the

BRIDES survey in 2007, discriminate against the poor. The poor are victims of the system because they lack the means to buy the desired verdict and because there is also no minimum administrative structure to make advance the system (*Le Nouvelliste,* 2018). This dysfunction of the judiciary, adds the newspaper, has led to a lack of proper justice, which has an adverse effect on the society at large.

- **Non-professionalization of public administration and low pay**

Regarding this fourth cause, *Le Nouvelliste,* citing IMF (2004), stipulates that with regard to the professionalization of public administration almost one in three public administration employees were 'phantasm' employees, and in some departments this proportion was as high as 50%. This crisis in Haitian public administration still persists because, according to the Office Management and Human Resources (OMRH), the state does not control the wage bill, does not know the workforce of its staff (*Le Nouvelliste*). This somber assessment leads to these rhetorical questions: who are collecting these issued checks? Are they fictitious individuals, former or dead employees? These checks are commonly referred to as "*chek zombi*" in Haitian Creole.

In regard to the recruitment of staff, *Le Nouvelliste* (2018) has quoted the coordinator of the OMHR as saying that public employees are recruited on the basis of clientelism and nepotism and that less than 5% of public service executives are licensed. The newspaper further indicates that in addition to the pitfalls of 'phantasm' employees and the lack of competence of non-phantasm executives, there is also the low wage sector, which encourages public servants to divert public funds to personal gain and discourages competent professionals from integrating the public administration. In reference to competence, there is a well-held view in the country that competence/qualification is less important than being a "political militant/activist".

In addition to the four above causes, this study will also consider four more factors that have contributed to the permanent state of corruption in the country.

- **"Grease the wheels"**

Like in most countries around the world (developed as well as developing), corruption has been an accepted practice in Haiti and "grease the wheels" has been one of its main features. Until recently, it had even been encouraged. The following sayings in the country capture the attitude toward corruption very well: (1) *Plumer la poule mais ne la laisser pas crier* (French); *Plimen poul la men pa kite l rele* (Haitian Creole), which literally means Pluck the chicken but don't let it make noise; (2) *Leta se chwal papa fok chak moun fe youn kou* (Haitian Creole), which is translated in English as "the State is our father's horse, each one of us has to take turn riding it". This second saying in part explains the state of political instability in the country in the sense that it encourages regime change so that another group of politicians come to power to ride the horse, meaning to embezzle funds and extort bribes. This view of the State also partially explains why the country had been a cradle for innumerous *coups d'état* throughout its history.

- **Political Instability**

As previously alluded to, political instability is another major cause of corruption in the country. Because government leaders know that they might not stay in power for a long period of time (except the two Duvaliers – Francois and Jean-Claude - who were determined to stay in power by all means, including the creation of the dreadful force : the *tontons macoutes*), they try to accumulate as much and as fast as possible while riding the horse. What makes this practice more damaging is the fact that the amount embezzled is sent overseas for safe-keeping and out of the reach of the Haitian people. These misappropriated funds could have been used for development projects or a social safety net for the disadvantaged.

- **Foreign Aid**

Haiti has been the recipient of a great deal of foreign aid (billions of dollars) for various reasons, including natural disasters, economic development, healthcare, and education, but this aid has not usually reached the people, especially the poor. In fact, foreign aid has been a major source of corruption in the country, and donors have been cognizant of this fact. Data released by the United Nations Office of the Special Envoy for Haiti (as of December 2012), and cited by https://www.lessonsfromhaiti.org, indicate that multilateral and bilateral donors have allocated $13.34 billion to relief and recovery efforts in Haiti for 2010 – 2012, and an estimated 48.2 percent ($6.43 billion) has been disbursed.

As the economic situation has not improved despite the enormous amount of aid, some analysts contend that Haiti has received too much foreign aid and asked where had the money gone. In this regard, James M. Roberts, a research fellow at The Heritage Foundation's Center for International Trade and Economics, argues that Haiti struggles with the insidious and negative effects of what could fairly be labeled as 'over-aid' from its developed friends, especially the United States. Since 2010, says Roberts (2015), hundreds of millions of dollars and dozens of metric tons of food have poured into Haiti from the United States.

The "massive quantities of food distributed by aid organizations" have undermined the country's agricultural production because "Haitian farmers growing staple foods… face disadvantages in cost versus imports subsidized rice from the U.S." (Roberts 2015). Being unable to compete with lower price of imported rice, many Haitian rice growers abandoned their farms and lost their source of livelihood (Germain, 2010). As domestic rice production declined, adds Germain (2010), and Haiti lacked financial means to import an adequate quantity of rice to satisfy domestic consumption, the country had to rely on food aid in terms of rice.

This perpetual dumping of foreign products ("food aid") – coupled with enormous amounts of foreign financial assistance - contributes not only to corruption and the destruction of the economy but also to the existence of a dependency syndrome at both the government and the population levels. That does not mean, however, that foreign assistance should be discontinued, but it should be utilized to accelerate the economic development process, which would mitigate aid dependency in the country. "Over-aid" is a misnomer. What is important is the manner in which the aid is utilized.

Regarding the 2010 earthquake in Haiti, billions of dollars were given to help the country recover from the disaster, but most of the funds were misused, and the people are still waiting for a meaningful change in their lives. Puzzled by what had happened, TIME (2011, January 10) posed this question: "How did such a huge outpouring of foreign assistance – donor countries have pledged some $11 billion – manage to accomplish so little"? TIME has provided an answer to its own question by stating that observers affixing blame tend to fall into one of two camps: those who point fingers at the armies of NGOs - 12,000 of them as of 2011 - working in Haiti; and those who fault the Haitians themselves.

Which one is the real culprit?

According to Ramachandra & Waltz (2012) of the Center for Global Development (CGD), since the 2010 earthquake almost $6 billion has been disbursed in official aid to Haiti and an estimated $3 billion has been donated to NGOs in private contributions in addition to official aid. The authors further indicate that non-governmental organizations (NGOs) and private contractors have been the intermediate recipients of most of these funds, and the Government of Haiti has received just 1 percent of humanitarian aid and somewhere between 15 and 21 percent of longer-term relief. By the way, the "armies" of NGOs are so influential and dominant that many Haitians and other observers refer to the country as the "Republic of NGOs" or the "NGO Republic of Haiti". This dominance is very problematic because it has further weakened the State. As the existence of a "parallel state" is abnormal and the NGOs should not be playing such a *de facto* role, Ramachandra & Waltz (2012, January 9) recommend that NGOs working in Haiti be asked to sign the equivalent of the Paris Declaration for aid donors – one that would require registration, coordination, and cooperation with the government. That would be an improvement because the Paris Declaration is organized around five principles designed to make aid more effective: ownership, alignment, harmonization, managing for results, and mutual accountability.

Despite the large amount of public funds donated to and channeled via the NGOs to circumvent corrupt national public officials, the outcomes are not noticeably better. Comparing the performance of the Haitian government to that of the NGOs, *America-The Jesuit Review* (2018, February 22) states, "Haiti has a reputation for corrupt government, but waste, mismanagement, fraud and corruption also plague charities, non-governmental organizations and aid agencies. Only a small fraction of the outside aid pledged to Haiti after the 2010 earthquake actually reached the Haitian people". An analysis of the afore-mentioned data (both quantitative and qualitative) should help the reader to answer the "blame" question. The real issue, however, should not be which one of the two entities is more at fault or more corrupt, but a demand for transparency, accountability, and better performance, which would go a long way to answer the perennial question "Where has all the money gone?". A result-oriented policy needs to be implemented especially because "aid agencies face poor incentives to deliver results and underinvest in enforcing aid conditions and performing scientific evaluations" (Easterly, 2010).

TIME (2011) has provided its own account of the earthquake funds by stating that (1) only around 10% of the funds committed to Haiti's recovery have actually been spent there; (2) aid contracts intended to provide work for Haitians have benefited foreign companies instead; (3) out of 1,500 U.S. contracts given out in 2010, only 20 went to Haitian-owned companies. This disconcerting account begs the question: Was the aid given to help economic recovery in Haiti or enrich the "armies" of NGOs and foreign contractors? This account also negates the 'over-aid' argument and corroborates this author's previous statements: "'Over-aid' is a misnomer. What is important is the manner in which the aid is utilized".

TIME further indicates that even before the quake, Haiti was home to more foreign aid workers than any other country on earth, and it is considered by many observers as a case study of the hypocrisy of the global relief bandwagon that descends on poor countries victimized by wars, famine and natural disasters. As a result, a growing chorus of critics accuses humanitarian-aid groups of using misery to validate their existence, spending funds inefficiently; the Haitian tragedy reflects a broader debate in foreign policy circles about the relationship between aid and development (TIME, 2011).

How to remedy the situation?

The dominance of international NGOs and private contractors in Haiti has created a parallel state more powerful than the government itself; these entities have built an alternative infrastructure for the provision of social services, but do not have much accountability (Ramachandra & Waltz, 2012). After acknowledging that the NGOs and private contractors will most likely continue to dominate service provisions in Haiti for some time to come, Ramachandra and Waltz recommend three options to improve the situation: 1) NGOs and private contractors carry out systematic and widely accessible evaluations of their work; 2) All actors in Haiti be held accountable by publishing data on expenditures and outcomes in Haiti; and 3) The Government of Haiti procure services through competitive bidding whenever possible, in order to maintain service delivery while building local capacity over the longer time. In respect to the second option, Ramachandra & Waltz assert that the International Aid Transparency Initiative (IATI) may be the perfect vehicle for this and the United States government should require NGOs (and possibly private contractors) to report to IATI, and IATI compliance might eventually be a prerequisite for receiving US funds.

The damning accounts by Roberts (2015), TIME (2011), Ramachandra & Waltz (2012), and America- The Jesuit Review (2018) in the case of Haiti appear to give credence to William Easterly 's argument that foreign aid is not conducive to development in the developing world. As to why, Easterly (2006) asserts that foreign aid does not work because the system keeps going back to the same failed ideas that prevent most aid money from actually reaching the world's poor. In addition to not reaching the poor, foreign aid has remained a source of corruption despite the fact that (in Haiti for example) international donors have bypassed corrupt public officials by channeling the funds through NGOs. The misappropriated billions of dollars in foreign aid could have contributed to growth and development, and a significant improvement in people's standard of living. As international donors - in this era of anti-corruption - have recognized the failure of foreign assistance and started demanding transparency and accountably, perhaps they will find a way to restrain those who are willing and able to transform poverty into a lucrative industry - the *poverty industry.*

As Haiti is the only country in the western world that has been on the list of the *least developed countries* (LDCs) since the inception of this category by the United Nations in 1971 (Germain, 2018), the "armies" of the 12,000 NGOs as of 2011 – operating in cooperation with the Government of Haiti - could use the "massive" foreign funds in a manner that is conducive to the removal of the country from the LDC category. Such a commitment and result- oriented approach would help to justify their presence in the country and the use of public funds. While suggesting the *graduation of Haiti from the LDC category* as a goal, this author is well aware of the fact that the role of most NGOs is usually to provide day-to-day (short-term) assistance to people and not to foster long-term development. The NGOs, however, are in a position to use their resources (human and financial) and influence to facilitate the development process, and contribute to the strengthening of national institutions by working in *cooperation* with the government, assuming the latter shares these goals.

Towards this new co-operation and to stress the importance of development, the author of this study suggests that the *Ministere de Planification et de Cooperation Externe* – better known as *Ministere du Plan* - (Ministry of Planning and External Cooperation) be renamed *Ministere de Developpemnt et de Cooperation Externe* (Ministry of Development and External Cooperation), which would be the lead Ministry and coordinator of all development activities under the umbrella of the Government.

A constructive collaboration between the government and *all* international aid entities working in Haiti is very important to achieve the *proposed* goal of graduating the country from the LDC group because development is not simply an economic issue; it is also a long-term process that requires political will and commitment, technical skills, and a measurable result-oriented national strategy (MeRONS). If the actions of all the agents (national as well as international) are not coordinated, the goal will not be achieved. Despite co-operation, however, the *desired* goal will remain unattainable if the *corruption* problem is not addressed and mitigated. As it is now universally recognized that corruption diverts resources needed for sustainable development, it is imperative to first control this systemic problem.

In making his proposal, this author also wants to acknowledge that in 2013 Haiti's Prime Minister and Minister of Planning and External Cooperation had prepared a "Three-Year-Investment Program and its Framework designed to achieve accelerated, balanced economic growth and reduce poverty… [and] to make Haiti an emerging country by 2030". The Program called on Haiti's development partners and donors in the international community to play a role "in our efforts to attain our objectives and in the development and reconstruction".

This author has mentioned the Three-Year-Investment Program not because of the Plan *per se,* but because of its ultimate goal of making "Haiti an emerging country", which coincides with his idea of graduating Haiti from the LDC group. For generations and generations, Haiti's *Ministere du Plan* had designed notorious *Plan Quinquennal* (Five-Year Plan) simply to "end up collecting dust in the Ministry's drawers". The Three-Year Investment Program attracts this author's attention because: (1) the goal of making "Haiti an emerging country" is laudable; (2) the Program was designed in consultation with the World Bank and the IMF based on these institutions' *Poverty Reduction Strategy (PRS) Initiative.* Germain (2018) has analyzed the PRS process in *Poverty Reduction in the Least Developed Countries.*

The Three-Year Investment Program, however, has a major fundamental flaw because it anticipates "strong economic growth… at rates approaching 10 percent, based on [*inter alia*] the creation of businesses, and foreign direct investment". As this paper has previously demonstrated, investors (foreign as well as domestic) are not likely to invest in a country where corruption is endemic. As investment and corruption are inversely correlated, particularly in highly corrupt low-income countries, priority one must be to *control corruption,* which would serve as a catalyst for change and development in the country. Although it is a complex and difficult task, this step cannot be skipped if the Government and the international community are really committed "to make Haiti an emerging country". Any attempt to avoid this prerequisite to development in Haiti will lead to the same result as the "massive" international aid mobilized after the 2010 earthquake. In other words, the new Development Plan will meet the same faith as the Plan of Action for the Recovery and Development of Haiti (PARDH), which was designed at the New York conference in March 2010 by the international community to provide support for the reconstruction of the country after the earthquake. Development and attainment of the goal of making Haiti an emerging country (meaning graduating Haiti from the LDC category) will occur via controlling corruption, as previously stated.

- **"Cash-only" Payment Rule**

In addition to the aforementioned causes of corruption in Haiti, Craig Mascarenhas (2017, March 27) has added the "cash-only" payment rule instituted by Customs officials based on his personal experience in the country. In August 2016, says Mascarenhas, he was part of a small project to engineer and build a clean water system in Haiti, which required importing equipment and supplies, and the items that his group was attempting to bring into the country were exempt from tax because of their use in non-commercial setting and in association with an NGO. Despite the fact that this was clearly stated on the Custom form, reports Mascarenhas, the Customs officials insisted that he paid tax on the products *in cash* directly to the Customs officer, without an option to make a payment to a government agency.

Mascarenhas further indicates that this was a common practice to extort cash at Haitian Customs, and the Haitian government was aware of the problem. Mascarenhas, however, acknowledges that in 2013 the government launched a general crackdown with a handful success, such as the arrest of a prominent Haitian businessman who was involved with multiple Customs officers in a ring that involves contraband and trafficking. According to him, the crackdown did not lead to a meaningful reduction in corrupt Customs practices. Mascarenhas' experience illustrates how entrenched is corruption and tends to support the view that corruption is more about networks than transactions by individual actors. Aware of the harmful effect of the illicit "cash-only" payment practice, Mascarenhas made three concrete proposals to remedy the problem: (1) replace the "cash-only" payment rule with a "no-cash" payment rule, making Customs taxes payable directly to a verified government body; (2) authorize external audits of Haitian Customs; and (3) out-source Haitian Customs.

In addition to the examined corrupt practices, Haitian governments had used several other techniques to collect payoffs. For example, between the 1910s and the 1970s in Haiti, goods such as expensive liquor were almost untaxed, but duties were high on cotton, textiles, soap, and kerosene (Lundahl, 1997). Rose-Ackerman & Palifka (2016) explain the rationale for this occurrence as follows: because tax breaks can be awarded to corrupt individuals and firms in return for bribes, kleptocrats may set high nominal tax rates to encourage payoffs and may set heavy duties on necessities used by the poor and exempt luxuries.

2.4. Consequences of Corruption in Haiti

Corruption in the forms of bribes, theft (financial and physical), and embezzlement, *inter alia,* has had disastrous impact on economic growth and development in the country. To illustrate this fact, this study will consider two examples: the Duvalier regime and the PetroCaribe scandal.

- **The Duvalier Regime**

PBS (2009) has given an account on one of Haiti's former president, which explains the extent to which corrupt officials have hindered the country's development. According to PBS, during the 15-year reign of Haiti's former president Jean-Claude 'Baby Doc' Duvalier 1971-1986, international aid organizations tried to help improve the country's economic situation, but Duvalier pocketed much of the relief money for himself. More specifically, PBS states that according to documents made available, shortly after the International Monetary Fund granted $22 million to Haiti on 5 December 1980, $20 million of that money was withdrawn from the government bank account, and approximately $4 million may have been diverted to Haiti's secret police while the remaining $16 million disappeared into Duvalier's personal accounts.

In an attempt to explain where the embezzled funds have gone, PBS reports that at the same time that the money went missing, Duvalier was making lavish purchases, like the eighty-foot luxury yacht, named 'Niki", that he bought for $1 million, and even after he fled the country in 1986 to escape an imminent coup, the spending continued. As an example of this lavish life style in exile, PBS mentions Duvalier villa's monthly rent of $40,000 in the French Riviera as having Ferrari sports cars in the driveway. PBS also adds that it is estimated that Jean-Claude Duvalier, his ex-wife Michele Bennet Duvalier and three agents are believed to have taken $504 million from the Haitian public between 1971 and 1986.

Jean-Claude Duvalier also misappropriated Haiti's public physical properties. In this respect, Fisman and Golden (2017) note that during his reign in the 1970s and 1980s, Jean-Claude Duvalier sold off the 150-kilometer rail link from Port-au-Prince (the capital in the West) to Verrettes [a city located at approximately 58 kilometer north of Port-au-Prince] to an investment consortium that carefully packed up the tracks and shipped them out of the country. They further indicate that Duvalier presumably deposited the proceed into a Swiss bank account, leaving the public without even the funds derived from destroying Haiti's transportation infrastructure.

Lundahl (1997) reports that under the Duvaliers [father and son], checks were simply written out to members of the presidential family and other private citizens from various state monopolies.

According to the U.S. Department of Commerce, state Rose-Ackerman & Palifka (2016), in 1977-8 Haitian government misappropriation of funds was 63% of government revenue. According to the authors, the dictatorial rule of Francois Duvalier and his son Jean-Claude Duvalier in Haiti (1957-1986) benefited just a few thousand people connected by marriage, family ties or friendship to those in power. Rose-Ackerman & Palifka further indicate that dictatorial governments in Haiti favored institutions that impeded development because they were the most effective way to siphon off rents in the Haitian context, and consequently the assets of the wealthy were invested either overseas or in secure, but unproductive, investment.

- **The PetroCaribe Scandal**

PetroCaribe refers to a fund set up by Venezuela's former president Hugo Chavez in 2005 to provide loans to other countries in the Caribbean, but the loan consists of oil instead of cash. Under the PetroCaribe accord signed in May 2006, Venezuela's state oil company sells oil to Haiti, which "has up to 90 days from the date of each delivery to pay Venezuela 60% of the bill " and allows the country to defer payments on the remaining 40% of the oil bought for up to 25 years, charging a low rate of one percent (1%) interest for the debt. The agreement also allows the Government of Haiti to sell the oil domestically and use the proceeds to finance development projects.

As people in Haiti had not seen the benefits from the program, they became suspicious and demanded an investigation. In November 2017, reports TIME (2019), a five-person commission in the Haitian Senate investigated the program and reported evidence of widespread corruption in the use of the funds under three successive governments; the Commission report indicates that the amount of money in government coffers was misreported, exchange rates were adjusted and more than half of the contracts given to companies to service the projects did not go through the usual government bid process. Furthermore, the Commission recommended that charges be brought against several former public officials.

In addition to the Senatorial Commission report, France Medias Monde (2019) posits that Haiti's Superior Court of Auditors added fuel to the fire when it issued its own report in January 2019 in which it cited disastrous management practices and the suspected diversion of nearly $2 billion from the PetroCaribe funds. This damaging report ignited the anger of the Haitian people and served as a catalyst for anti-corruption activists, who called themselves "PetroCaribe Challengers", to launch a grassroots movement against ubiquitous corruption in the country.

The embezzlement of the PetroCaribe funds has negatively impacted the Haitian people in two major ways: first, they have not benefited from the proceeds of the "oil loans" as intended, and second, the country (meaning the people) is obligated to repay the loans to Venezuela, which has added to the country's debt burden. The misappropriation of the PetroCaribe proceeds by public officials brings to light a dichotomy not only in Haiti but also in many other countries. These officials usually (sometimes rightfully) complain about international aid "conditionalities" imposed on them by donors, but when the aid comes *without* preconditions or oversight - such as the PetroCaribe assistance program – corrupt actors tend to embezzle the aid. That raises a serious question of credibility and accountability.

The prevalence of corruption in public administration has led the people to mistrust government in general, especially the judicial system, which has served as a rationale for many citizens to take the law into their own hands and give themselves "popular justice". This *modus operandi* has had adverse effects on the proper functioning of the country's society. Moreover, the existence of a high level of corruption denies the people access to essential services because they are often required to pay bribes in order to obtain those services.

In terms of the economy, the high level of corruption has had disastrous impact on growth and development because it has led to a decrease in investment (foreign and domestic) and job creation. Companies and entrepreneurs that would be willing to invest in Haiti have opted to invest elsewhere to avoid the high costs of doing business in the country. Government officials who expect the wheels to be "greased" (known in Haiti as "grease my hands") delay the approval process for proposed business projects in order to collect bribes. A process that could have taken days might take months, even years (if ever approved). This technique to collect bribes is not unique to Haiti; it is a common practice used by corrupt government officials across the globe.

Evaluating the costs of corruption in Haiti, Nazario (2007) indicates that the effect of improving political corruption ratings by 1.0 unit of measure for Haiti would potentially increase the gross national product (GNP) by 206 percent, capital by US$ 5 billion, foreign direct investments (FDI) by US$ 800 million, and domestic savings by US$ 2.3 billion.

CHAPTER 3
CITIZENS' REACTIONS TO CORRUPTION

3.1. Demand for Accountability

Disillusioned by the PetroCaribe scandal, Haitians started asking "where is the PetroCaribe money?". They took to the streets demanding the resignation of President Jovenel Moise amid allegations he embezzled hundreds of thousands of dollars of government funds earmarked for badly needed social programs (TIME, 2019). They also demanded an independent investigation because they do not trust government officials. France Medias Monde (2019) quoted Pascale Solages, a protester, as saying, "Corruption means the administration is filled by senators, lawmakers who use their positions to nominate their friends, their families, people without experience or expertise".

One of the reasons for demanding the resignation of President Moise is that allegations of corruption against him had surfaced even before he was sworn in. In this regard, TIME (2019) indicates that the published report on the PetroCaribe investigation alleges that Moise helped embezzle funds from a large PetroCaribe project before he came to office when he was head of the company Agricans;

and the company was paid around $700,000 to repair some road even though its entire business was growing bananas.

As anger grew over the alleged misuse of the PetroCaribe funds, protests by thousands and thousands of people throughout the country turned violent. Protesters blocked roads and burned tires to demand more transparency in how the government uses funds from PetroCaribe (AP News 2018, October 17). They argue that the savings from the agreement with Venezuela were supposed to fund sustainable social projects and strategic investments to help with development.

The Haiti Branch of Transparency International (2018, July 25) has called on the executive and legislative powers to reduce their lavish lifestyle. They argue that Haitian Senators and *Deputes* [House Representatives] in Parliament and members of the government live well above the economic reality of the country with advantages and privileges that go beyond understanding.

3.2. A Diplomatic *Faux Pas*

Surprisingly, the Special Representative of the United Nations Secretary-General and Chief of the UN Mission for Justice Support in Haiti (MINUJUSTH), Susan D. Page, released a statement in which she said, "I welcome the initiative and the active role of Haitian citizens and civil society who are in the fight against corruption and impunity… their actions demonstrate that the population is standing up for accountability and justice".

According to *Haiti Observateur* (2018, November 14), Haiti's Foreign Minister reacted by saying, "Ms. Page exceeded her authority by welcoming an investigation into the alleged misuse of Venezuela-sponsored PetroCaribe funds by the Haitian previous administrations. Ms. Page reportedly made an applaud on the corruption inquiry into the alleged siphoning $2 billion oil loans from Venezuela as PetroCaribe money…Ms. Page's attitude is harmful to the political and institutional stability acquired during the past few years", and the government demanded an explanation. The Government seized on the statement to silence the UN Representative. It considered the press release as a "criticism" of the government, which was behind the use of the phrases "exceeded her authority", "harmful to the political and institutional stability". In this context, the UN Representative's statement was viewed as a diplomatic *faux pas*.

As "the UN has its own terrible track record in terms of avoiding accountability for its actions [in the country] ", President Moise used the controversy to the utmost by playing the "nationalist" card. Some analysts and critics wondered whether he was defending the country's interest or the corrupt political system as he was himself accused of embezzling part of the PetroCaribe funds. They argued that his name (among other top officials) was mentioned in the report of the Senate Commission on the PetroCaribe misappropriated funds. Regardless the President's motivation, the result of the controversy over the press release was that Ms. Page had to "travel" to the UN Headquarters in New York. This diplomatic incidence had mixed reactions in the country, which led to the question: Is a UN statement welcoming the investigation of corrupt activities a "criticism" of the government or a "support" for accountability? Regardless the answer to this complex question, the incidence does reveal the intricacy of combating corruption, even under UNCAC's umbrella.

CHAPTER 4

NATIONAL ANTI-CORRUPTION MEASURES

4.1. The Executive Branch

After months of nationwide street protests by citizens demanding transparency, investigation, and accountability from the government regarding misappropriations of the PetroCaribe funds, President Moise promised to investigate the allegations, and "hold all of those responsible accountable". According to AFP (2019, February 17), Prime Minister Jean-Henry Cean announces that government officials will lose their perks under emergency economic and anti-corruption measures, and he promises to cut the prime minister's budget by 30 percent. This decision was interpreted as a signal sent by the prime minister to the presidency and the parliament to do the same. AFP also quotes the prime minister as saying, "We also need to withdraw all unnecessary privileges for high-level governments like allowances for gas and telephones, needless trips abroad, and the number of consultants".

4.2. The Legislative Branch

The Haitian Parliament finally passed an anti-corruption legislation on 11 March 2014. According to Nicolai Behr (2014, May 16)

- an attorney and a member of the committee "International" of the German Institute for Compliance - non-governmental organizations were asked to provide input for the new anti-corruption law from the beginning of the process. As such, adds Behr, the enacted rules are based on Transparency International's Source Book which has been adapted to the specific Haitian context. The new anti-corruption legislation, continues Behr, defines corruption broadly to criminalize nepotism, the passing of insider information on procurement procedures, and sexual harassment in the process of employment; the law also provides rules that resolve conflicts of interest in awarding contracts.

Some skeptics wonder how this new legislation will be enforced, especially the clause "decreeing a national zero-tolerance policy" toward corruption. As corruption is viewed as a global phenomenon that is difficult (if not almost impossible) to eradicate, the skeptics also wonder whether the legislation is enforceable (zero tolerance), or is simply a façade to placate the critics, or whether the Parliament was compelled to adopt it because of pressure from the international community to comply with the UN Convention against Corruption whose Article 17 unambiguously addresses the issue of "*Embezzlement, misappropriation or other diversion of property by a public official*". Article 17 does require "Each State Party" of the Convention to criminalize those corrupt activities.

Whatever the reason, the anti-corruption legislation is a welcome step toward accountability. With regard to its implementation, the Haiti's Chapter of Transparency International holds this view: "Our new anti-corruption law is a good one. It's now up to the government to implement it. Making sure this happens will be our next challenge".

In addition to passing an anti-corruption legislation, a Senate's Special Commission of Investigation issued a 656-page report in November 2017 detailing alleged embezzlement and fraud by current and former Haitian officials managing $2 billion in loans from Venezuela's PetroCaribe discounted oil-program from 2008 and 2016 (U.S. Congressional Research Service, 2019). As public pressure mounted after the people became aware of the report, President Moise fired "two high-ranking officials in his government for their involvement in the scandal".

4.3. Current State of the Government in Haiti

Amid tensions between the executive and the legislature, parliamentary elections scheduled for October 2019 did not take place. As a result of the government's failure to hold these elections, the terms of most members of the Haitian legislature expired on January 13, 2020, which renders the parliament dysfunctional. As of this date, the President has been ruling the country by decree, which is a concern for many citizens because of the country's history of brutal dictatorship and *coups d'état*. Critics argue that President Moise has used the opportunity to dissolve the Parliament as a means to bypass the legislature and neutralize his political opponents, who immediately condemned the rule by decree. The Parliament being dissolved, President Moise unilaterally named an unratified new prime minister to lead "a government of transparency and consensus".

Nevertheless, thousands and thousands of people continue to hold mass demonstrations and demand President Moise's resignation. According to the U.S. Congressional Research Service (2020), the judiciary is conducting ongoing investigations into Moise's possible involvement in various corrupt activities, which he continues to deny.

4.4. Proposed Anti-Corruption Strategy

To combat corruption in Haiti, Klitgaard (2010) has suggested a very elaborate strategy that includes the following ideas: (1) the President announces that all public officials sign a simple code of conduct, which precludes the acceptance of bribes; (2) the President declares that no one will be allowed to bid on a public contract who has not signed a similar standard of conduct concerning the offering of bribes; (3) the public sector will be enlisted to form an independent monitoring capability to follow up complaints; (4) international organizations offer financial support for such investigations, including by international NGOs and investigative firms; (5) the President announces an experimental program within the Customs Agency and the Tax Bureau; if revenues in the next year exceed a certain target increase, a small portion of that increase will go to employees of these agencies as a bonus; (6) the President announces publicly that the country will conduct some number of 'sting' operations during the next year, among other new ideas.

Klitgaard's proposed strategy is apropos and innovative in Haiti's context. If implemented, it would go a long way to mitigate the enduring problem of corruption, but there is a caveat. It revolves too much around the country's president. The proposed strategy appears to imply that the sitting President is above the systemic corrupt practices that permeate the public sector. As corruption has been endemic and "grease the wheels" has been a *modus operandi* and *modus vivendi* in the country, what would happen if the president is an integral part of the problem?

Would he or she be willing and able to implement the strategy? In this regard, World Bank (2017) contends that changes in formal rules and anticorruption strategies are likely to be enforced only when they are aligned with the interests of powerful actors in a country.

Remember the allusion made in section 1 to the case of President Lula of Brazil who initiated anti-corruption measures and ended in prison himself after the expiration of his terms in office. Should a proposed strategy to combat corruption also include a worldwide moratorium for corrupt activities that preceded the adoption of the UN Convention against Corruption? Or the date UNCAC went into force? Or any other relevant date with certain provisos?

The experience of the UN Representative Susan Page and that of the former Prime Minister Pierre-Louis previously discussed reveal the complexity of fighting systemic corruption in the country, but combating corruption is a *sine qua non* condition for growth and development in Haiti. To foster development, the relationship between the governing body and the governed must go through some changes. Francois "Papa Doc" Duvalier – soon after acceding to the presidency in 1957 - described that relationship as follows: "The country is split into two groups: the *exploiters* (emphasis) - restless and foolhardy minority – monopolize the administrative power and paralyze the progress of the masses; the *exploited* (emphasis) – the great majority – [are] victims of a wrongly and cruel system" (Ramachandra & Walz, 2012). This prevailing relationship impedes the development process. The control of corruption would be a gigantic step towards the required systemic changes. In Haiti's context, however, the attainment of this desired goal will not occur without external political and economic cooperation because Haiti's political system has been dominated by outside forces for more than two centuries. The country's tumultuous history is a testament to the interconnectedness between the national and the international.

CHAPTER 5

CONCLUSION

This paper has investigated the impact of corruption on growth and development, and examined the measures adopted and actions taken or proposed to mitigate the negative effects of corruption at both global and a country-specific levels. After justifying the assumption made on the linkage between corruption and development, it has examined the causes and consequences of corruption at the global level, and also the actions taken by the international community, particularly Transparency International, and the United Nations.

The study finds that corruption has had disastrous impact on the world's economies. It costs the world economy an estimated $1 trillion paid in bribes *every year* and $26 billion *annually* in stolen funds. The study also finds that corruption hinders economic growth and development in a variety of ways: 1) it discourages foreign and domestic investment by increasing opportunity for rent-seeking, creating uncertainty, and reducing incentives for investors; 2) it harms economic efficiency; 3) it adversely impacts economic performance by lowering productivity of the factors of production; 3) it significantly increases investors' costs of doing business; 4) it diverts funds intended to provide essential services; 5) it deters innovation by reducing economic growth in the long run; 6) it has a debilitating effect on development in countries rich in natural resources; 7) it exacerbates poverty and negatively impacts economic growth; 8) it encourages tax evasion, which lowers governments' revenues; 9) it leads to weak governance, which impedes governments' ability to implement policies conducive to growth and development; 10) it diverts precious resources needed for sustainable development.

The study also shows that corruption "sands the wheels" of economic growth and development instead of "greasing" them.

More surprisingly, the study finds that the amount of money extorted and stolen each year in developing countries is over 10 times the approximately $100 billion in foreign assistance being provided to them by all governments and civil society organizations in the world.

To mitigate the negative effects of corruption at the global level, some conventions have been adopted and agreements reached, including the United Nations Convention against Corruption, the World Bank Group's International Corruption Hunters Alliance, Inter-American Convention against Corruption, Organisation for Economic Co-operation and Development's Convention on Combatting Bribery of Foreign Public Officials in International Business, African Union Convention on Preventing and Combatting Corruption, and Financial Action Task Force (FATF) on Money Laundering.

At the country level, the paper finds that theft of financial resources has been the main tool used by government officials in Haiti to divert funds that could have been used to improve people's quality of life through the implementation of social programs and development projects. In 1977-8, for example, Haitian government misappropriation of funds was 63% of government revenues.

It also finds that governments in Haiti has favored institutions that impeded development because they were the most effective way to siphon off rents.

To substantiate the findings regarding the specific case of Haiti, the study has explicitly examined two cases of corruption: the Duvalier's and the PetroCaribe scandal, and found that an estimated $504 million and $2 billion were, respectively, embezzled. The magnitude of the amount misappropriated in these two cases alone underscores the prevalence of corruption in the country and its adverse impact on people, society, and the economy. In addition to financial theft, the study also found that the high cost of doing business in Haiti – due to corruption - had discouraged companies from investing in the country, which had hindered job creation and development.

The study also reveals that improving political corruption by 1.0 unit of measure for Haiti would potentially increase the gross national product (GNP) by 206 percent, capital by US$ 5 billion, foreign direct investment (FDI) by US$ 800 million, and domestic savings by US$ 2.8 billion.

With regard to actions taken at the country level, the Haitian Parliament passed an anti-corruption legislation that criminalized nepotism, the passing of insider information on procurement procedures, among other sanctions. The new legislation also includes a clause "decreeing a national zero-tolerance" to corruption.

In terms of solutions, the adoption of UNCAC, which requires countries to criminalize certain practices - including financial theft - represents a very significant step toward at least a reduction in corruption at the global and national levels. The adoption of anti-corruption measures, if enforced, could serve as a deterrent to corruption, and a disincentive to use "grease the wheels" as a common practice. It would also make government officials more accountable and responsive to the needs of people.

Concerning the effectiveness of the anti-corruption measures adopted, and whether they will significantly mitigate the impact of corruption on development, it is too soon to provide a valid evaluation. But the alarms have been activated, and part of the massive amount of stolen funds has been recovered and returned to the countries of origin.

REFERENCES

AFP (2019, February 17). "Haiti officials to lose perks in PM's response to violent unrest". Retrieved from https://news.yahoo.com/haiti-officials-to-lose-perks-pms-response-to-violent-unrest-091459006.html

America-The Jesuit Review (2018, February 22). "Are N.G.O.s in Haiti doing more harm than good". Retrieved from https://www.americamagazine.org/politics-society/2018/02//22/are-ngos-haiti/doing-more-harm-good.

AP (2018, October 17). "Haitians protest alleged misused of PetroCaribe funds". Retrieved from https://apnews.com/87b6c953f8cf4bfa828451d9c741369

Behr, N (2014, May16). "Haitian Parliament passes anti-corruption legislation." Retrieved from https://globalcompliancenews.com/haitian-parliament-passes-anti-corruption-legislation.

CSIS (2018, November 29). "An Anatomy of Corruption: Haiti". Retrieved from https://www.csis.org/analysis/anatomy/corruption-haiti

De Souza Martins, J. (1996). "Clientelism and corruption in Contemporary Brazil", chapter 9 in Little, W. & Posada-Carbo, E. (eds) *Political Corruption in Europe and Latin America,* London,

Macmillan/Institute of Latin American Studies, University of London, pp.195-218.

Easterly, W. (2010). "Can Foreign Aid Buy Growth". Retrieved from https://williameasterly.files.wordpress/2010/08/04_easterly_canforeignaidbuygrowth_prp.pdf.

Easterly, W. (2016, November 27). "Aid Effectiveness: A Debate Between Steve Radelet and William Easterly". Center for Global Development. Retrieved from https://www.cgdev.org/blog/aid-effectiveness-debate-between-steve-radelet-and-william-easterly.

Finan & Ferraz (2005, November 16)." Exposing Corrupt Politicians: The Effect of Brazil's Publicly Released Audits on Electoral Outcomes". Retrieved from https://escholarship.org/uc/item/86n8r3pc.

Fisman, R & Golden, M.A (2017). *Corruption: What Everyone Needs to Know.* UK: University Press.

Fitzsimons, V.G. (2007). "Economic Model of Corruption". In *Corruption and Development: The Anti-Corruption Campaigns.* Sarah Bracking (ed.). UK: Palgrave Macmillan.

Foreign Policy (2013, July 16). "The Surprising Relationship Between Corruption and Economic Growth". Retrieved from https://foreignpolicy.com/2013/07/16/the-surprising-relationship-between-corruption-and- economic-growth/

Klitgaard, R. (2010, February). "Addressing Corruption in Haiti". Retrieved from https://groups.google.com/d/topic/haiti-nation/4M7R6xh96eQ.

Flitgaard, R. (1998, March). "International Cooperation Against Corruption". In *Finance & Development.* Washington, D.C: International Monetary Fund.

Flitgaard, R. (1988). *Controlling Corruption.* Los Angeles, CA: University of California Press.

France Media Monde (2019, February 15). "PetroCaribe Challenge: The Campaign mobilizing Haitians against corruption". Retrieved from https://www.france24.com/en/20190215-petrocaribe-challenge-social-media-campaign

Germain, JC. (2010). *Trade Liberalization and Globalization: The Experience of Haiti.* Ann Harbor, MI: UMI Publishing.

Germain, JC. (2018). *Poverty Reduction in the Least Developed Countries.* Munich: GRIN Verlag.

Government of the Republic of Haiti (2013, June). "2014-2016 Three-Year Investment Program and its Framework". Port-au-Prince, Haiti.

Gupta, S., Davoodi, H., & Tiongson, E. (2000). "Corruption and the Provision of Healthcare and Educational Services". Retrieved from http://www.imf.org/external/pubs/ft/wp/2000/wp00116.pdf

Krugman, P. R. & Obstfeld, M. (2006). *International Economics.* New York: Pearson, Addison Wesley.

Haiti Observateur (2018, November 14). "Senior U.N. Official Cheering an Investigation Over Misuse of PetroCaribe Funds". Retrieved from www.haiti.observer.com/blog/sector/u-n--official-cheering-an-investigation-over-misuse-of-PetroCaribe-funds.

Lambsdorff, J.G. (2007). *The Institutional Economics of Corruption and Reform.* Cambridge, U.K: Cambridge University Press.

Le Nouvelliste (2018, November 27). "*Corruption et administration publique en Haiti: Causes et Solutions*". Retrieved from https://lenouvelliste.com/article/195277/corruption-et-administration-publique- en-haiti-causes-et-2017solutions.

Lundahl, M. (1997). "Inside the Predatory State: The Rationale, Methods, and Economic Consequences of Kleptocratic Regimes" in *Nordic Journal of Political Economy* 24: 31-50.

Mascarenhas, C (2017, March 27). "Cracking Down on Corruption in Haitian Customs". Retrieved from https://globalanticorruptionblog.com/tag/Haiti.

Mauro, P. (1995). "Corruption and Growth". Retrieved from http://elsa.berkeley.edu-saez/course131/Mauro95.pdf

Nazario, O. (2007). "A Strategy Against Corruption". Retrieved from www.casals.com.

PBS (2009). "Haiti: The Long Road to Recovery". Retrieved from https://pbs.org/frontlineworld/stories/bribe/2009/05/haiti-the-long-road-to-recovery

Ramachandra, V. & Walz, J. (2012, January 9). "Is Haiti Doomed to be the Republic of NGOs?". Retrieved from https://www.cgddev.org/blog/haiti-doomed-be-republic-ngos.

Ramachandra, V. & Walz, J. (2012, May). "Haiti: Where Has All the Money Gone?". Retrieved from http://www.cgdev.org/sites/default/files/1426185_file_Ramachandra_Walz_Haiti_Final_O.pdf

Roberts, J.M. (2015, December 18). "The Negative Effects on Haiti of Too Much Foreign Aid". Retrieved from https://www.dailysignals.com/2015/12/18/the-negative-effects-on-hati-of-too-much- foreign-aid/

Rose-Ackerman, S. & Palifka, B.J. (2016). *Corruption and Government.* New York: Cambridge University Press.

Stephenson, M. (2014, May 27). "Klitgaard 's Misleading 'Corruption Formula'". Retrieved from https://globalanticorruptionblog/2014/05/27klitgaards-corruption-formula/

Tanzi, V. & Davoodi, H. (2000). "Corruption, Growth and Public Finances". Retrieved from http://www.imf.org/external/pubs/ft/wp/2000/wp00182.pdf.

The New York Times (2020, January 15). "Trump Tried to Kill Anti-Bribery Rule He Deemed 'Unfair'". From www.nytimes.com

World Bank (2020, February 19). "Factsheet". Retrieved from https://blogs.world.org/en/news/factsheet/2020/02/19/anti-corruption-fact-sheet.print.

TIME (2011, January 10). "Who Failed on Haiti's Recovery". Retrieved from www.content.time.com/time/printout/0.8816.2041450.00.html

TIME (2019, June 24). "Haiti Protests: What is PetroCaribe and Why is it Fueling". Retrieved from https://www.tome.com/5609054/haiti-protests-petroCaribe.

Todaro, M. P. & Smith, S. C. (2017). *Economic Development.* India: Pearson Media Ltd.

Transparency International (2014). "The Impact of Corruption on Growth and Inequality". Retrieved from https://transparency.org/files/content/corruptiom-growth-and-inequality-2014-pdf

Transparency International (2018). "Haiti – Corruption Perceptions Index". Retrieved from https://knoema.com/atlas/haiti/corruption-perceptions-index

Transparency International Haiti Branch (2018, July 25). "Transparency International wants Haitians in power to reduce their lavish lifestyle". Retrieved from www.belpolitik.com/blog.transparency-international-wants-haitians-in-power-to- reduce-their-lavish-lifestyle.

Transparency International (2019). "CPI 2019: Global Highlights". Retrieved from https://www.transparency.org/news/feature/cpi_2019_global_highlights.

UNDP (2008, December)." Corruption and Development: Anti-Corruption Interventions for Poverty Reduction". United Nations Development Programme. Retrieved from www.undp.org/governance.

UNODC (2016). "Corruption and Development: International Anti-Corruption Day". United Nations Office on Drug and Crime. Retrieved from https://www.anticorruption.org/documents/actagainstcorruption/print/materials2016

UNDOC (2019)." United Nations Convention against Corruption". Retrieved from https://www.unodc.org/en/corruption/uncac.html

U.S. Congressional Research Service (2019, July 1). "Haiti's Political and Economic Conditions". Retrieved from https://crsreports.congress.gov.

U.S. Congressional Research Service (2020, March 5). "Haiti's Political and Economic Conditions". Retrieved from https://crsreports.congress.gov R45034.

Weil, D.N. (2014). *Economic Growth.* New York: Routledge World Bank (1997), September. "Helping Countries Combat Corruption: The Role of the World Bank". Retrieved from https://www1.worldbank.org/publicsector/anticorruption/cor02.html

World Bank (2017). *World Development Report 2017.* Washington D.C: The World Bank

World Bank Group (2020). *Going Broke.* Washington D.C: The World Bank.

Yikona, S. et al. (2011, December 6). "How corruption and tax evasion distort development". Retrieved from blogs.worldbank.org/governance/how-corruption-and-tax-evasion-distort-development.

Made in United States
North Haven, CT
04 November 2026

21763084R00050